AND SHADOW REMAINED

KEN FEB 28 2016 AN

PAVEMENT SAW PRESS
OHIO

Editor & Layout : David Baratier
Associate Editor: Sean Karns
Cover Design: Kathy McInnis
Duck Logo: Joe Napora

Grateful acknowledgment is made to the editors of the following jour-
nals in which these poems, or versions of these poems, first appeared:
5 A.M., Black Bear Review, Blue Mesa Review, Borderlands, Cape Rock,
Chiron Review, Connecticut River Review, Convolvulus, Crucible,
Explorations, Exquisite Corpse, Eye Rhyme, First Circle, Flyway, Lucid
Stone, The MacGuffin, Many Mountains Moving, Marlboro Review,
Nerve Cowboy, New Delta Review, Nightsun, Northeast Corridor, Old
Red Kimono, Owen Wister Review, Painted Hills Review, Pavement
Saw, Piedmont Literary Review, Poet Lore, River King Poetry,
Sou'wester, Stringtown, Troubadour, Way Station, Weber Studies,
Westview, Willow Review, Wordwrights, Writers' Forum, Zone 3.

Pavement Saw Press
PO Box 6291
Columbus, OH 43206
pavementsaw.org

Ohio Arts Council
∧ A STATE AGENCY
THAT SUPPORTS PUBLIC
PROGRAMS IN THE ARTS

Products are available through the publisher or:
SPD / 1341 Seventh St.
Berkeley, CA 94710 / 800.869.7553

CONTENTS

VI

I

WILD RICE MEDLEY

First, be easy on yourself—don't worry
about proportion, temperature, time,
about hard-to-please family, friends,
your own expertise and practicality.

Second, stay out of the way—let wild
and brown rice, mushroom and onion, walnut
and almond, sherry and soy sauce, butter
and black pepper come on their own as guests.

Third, let the ingredients putter at the stove—
the rices will boil in their separate pots,
the vegetables and nuts sauté in a pan.
Mixed in a bowl, they'll all oven-bake awhile.

Last, open wine. Serve salad. Maybe turkey,
salmon, moose. The recipe is foolproof,
guaranteed. Though, to be perfectly safe,
invite the mouth, that stranger, to explain.

A House Like Mine

The mother, robe wrapped tight,
sat in the kitchen, smoked Trues
as she worried a crossword,
radio tuned to the news.

The child was three. Swirly snow
blanked the small dogwood
and maple. Exhaling, the mother
didn't think what she should

or shouldn't be doing. A puzzle
like this soothed her, let her forget.
Tobacco felt so smoky-good
in her throat. Noon. Yet,

despite storm, all was right
in the world. An almost smile.
Her boy played quietly nearby.
Her man would be at work awhile.

FAMILY PHOTO

Granddad's poised
      in the shade of the eaves,
forefinger on shutter,
      viewing eldest grandson,
Kenneth, stooped
      picking the biggest
mushroom in the yard.
      Granddad snaps:
Kenneth, mushroom,
      plum tree trunk,
garden edge,
      snake.

SUFFERING SUCCOTASH

Mealtime? Ghastly. She was six,
littlest at the table, a mimic
of the father who hid himself
behind the news. The mother
sat complaining about cystitis,
a migraine, or else some exotic
four or five-syllable condition.
The brother ate his beans and corn
from a penknife which he thrust
down his throat like a midget
sword-swallower. The parents dug
into the meatloaf. The girl coughed.
A lazy universe turned away.

SPAM SONNET

To write fourteen lines on that storied meat
I recall mornings my dad scrambled it
with eggs. No bacon for pop. Just a bit
of that odd solid mass cooked on high heat,
mixed with onion and green pepper. Six feet
five inches tall, dad gripped that big skillet
with one hand, cracked eggs with the other. "Come get it,"
he'd shout, dishing the scramble. "Now eat,"
he'd command. Vomit, I thought. Ugly puke,
I thought. The taste of farting, I thought.
When I could, I fed it to our dog, Luke,
though I didn't know why oh why I taught
the pup to love the stuff. It was so sad.
Poor Luke. Got used to Spam—as had my dad.

CARPOOLING TO RODEPH SHALOM

Their week, the mother took the Chevy wagon,
loaded the son tight beside her up front,
then piled in the Levys, the Jacobys,
the Rosenbergs, the little Goldfarb boy
with his runny nose, before negotiating
her cryptic cross-suburb route, a tangle
of winding indirection that made no map-sense,
but did bypass the stress of Sunday morning
expressway traffic, that on-ramp migraine
she'd drive ten extra minutes to avoid.

The mother, intrepid worrier, had given up
this day for them: a packed car of royally bored
spoiled kids who were growing into the clones
of their parents, upper-middle-class Jews
who didn't think shit of spirit or God.
Returning home through Elkins Park, Ogontz,
Springfield, Flourtown, the mother celebrated
the end of those wasted drives by lighting
a cigarette, filling the air with smoke,
fingernails on steering wheel clicking her coda.

THE PHILADELPHIA HUNGRY

My father, big sports fan,
loved the Sunday buffet—
the omelets, bagels, salmon,
roast beef—and having me,
his son, to show off
for the customers. Next,
our full-stomached march
to the car, the short drive
to the cut-rate stadium lot
where he parked by the exit,
already thinking getaway.
As we walked to the seats,
he'd mutter under his breath
about conference rivals:
Redskins—ugly political town;
Giants—from the New York hellhole;
Cardinals—beer-drinking louts;
Cowboys—where Kennedy was shot.
From our upper-deck seats,
taking time out for soft pretzels,
peanuts, a second-half hot dog
with extra-large Coca-Cola,
we booed and cheered like the rest,
me, the customers, and my father,
salesman signalling a vendor for more.

Depression Glass

You broke three this month,
your grandparents' perfect
green-tinted dessert plates,
the ones you inherited
last fall because only you,
of the grandchildren, knew why
those dishes remained unused—
and only you had the will
to undo the secret

curse of the legacy. Yes,
your family history, a house
of untouched sweets, unopened
preserves, copious and dreary
swill. Those past lives had
hooks in your bone: the denial
of needs, the ruin of dreams,
the steady pursuit of death.
One last piece of glass to go.

JULY VISIT EAST

Sitting in the living room with my old man,
watching the Phils, top of the ninth,
the Pirates push across the lead run—
bunt single, passed ball, wild pitch,
suicide squeeze. "A ridiculous rally," I say,
expecting my father to smile, nod. Instead
his head rolls, neck jerks at the windpipe.
He begins to snore. I listen to the hoarse
shudder, study the swollen belly,
the jowls, the whisker stubs, the pouches
under the eyes. He looks like his father
looked the last time I saw him
alive. "Ugly," my father suddenly says,
peering. The man does not recognize me.
Filmy eyes protrude like a toad's.
"Ugly," he repeats, blinking once, twice.
Gray, opaque eyes. His head jolts,
a leash pulled. Again he snores.

I rush to the kitchen. My mother,
done with dinner dishes, gabs on the phone,
chainsmokes. Quickly through, I push open
the door to dark heat, suffocating air.
almost a hundred degrees, no moon, stars,
fireflies. Houselights behind me,
I'm down the steps, the driveway, running
down the road. Underfoot's soft,
slightly springy. I can smell asphalt
giving, pitch breaking down, old rubber.
I taste tar. Sprinting hard, not ripping
the hot blackness, I gulp humidity,
let the heaviness drape. At the bottom
of the hill, an intersection. I stop,
stand in the exact middle, put hands to knees,
gasp, jump. Coming right at me,
a car backfiring, one headlight burnt,
my old man dead at the wheel.

SELLING BOOKS, CHAPEL HILL

After work I'd walk along
West Rosemary, past Breadman's,
Tijuana Fats, Cat's Cradle,
Dip's, and into Carrboro
where I followed the railroad
tracks north. On clear nights,
once I passed Carr Mill,
I'd dawdle home, identifying
constellations. Cloudy nights
I'd stargaze uselessly,
that dense Carolina sky hovering
above. Either way I'd cut
through Fitch's lumberyard.
There one June night,
I drank with a girlfriend
atop a rotted pile
of throwaway plywood,
waiting for a meteor
that never showed.

December that year
I kept walking home angry.
30, 20, 15 degrees,
and for three weeks
peered into railroad ties,
counting them, thinking not stars,
but stories, all the stories
I might someday write,
would someday write . . .
if only . . . if only . . .
what? . . . what? . . .

That December, cutting
through Fitch's lumberyard,
I'd grind my heel
in the dirt, spit,
mutter those words
my mother had taught me

never to say. *Fucking*
motherfucking bitch.
You whore you. Shit.
The woodstove was always out,
my little house always cold.
In the dark I'd have to chop
kindling, carry it in
before I could stoke the stove,
light it, wait for heat. *Motherfucking*
cunt. I'll show you. Warm up.
When the fire caught
I'd shove in more wood
until flames rose and pipes hissed.
Serves you right. Asshole.

One night I arrived home
to find everything warm.
Friends had visited,
made a fire, left me
a Christmas invitation.
I had just missed them.
I checked the stove—still burning—
and as I opened the door wider
to add two splintered oak chunks,
a chip, curling red, shot out
and died. Suddenly I had to
suppress tears, couldn't,
so I cried into my pillow,
the house growing hotter,
my noises more guttural.

I slept without dreams,
with less anger that holiday.
There was somewhere to go.

SLEEPWALKER

One night, housesitting, having fallen
asleep in one room, he woke
upstairs in another, no memory
of the switch, but of a movie
which he'd dreamed in fast-motion,
his bar mitzvah birthday, thirteen,
him playing boy turned Torah-reading
rabbi gibbering in broken Hebrew,
a vast synagogue of the absurd.

Next, the reception, scary strangers—
mostly relatives—stepping forward
to furtively slip thin envelopes
in the breast pocket of his suit.
For hours he circled the party
morose, pouty star of this grainy
coming-of-age film. According
to script, he knew what it meant
to be Jewish, and a man.

OUR DEVELOPMENT

My father bought early
and cheap, a small
wooden house, almost
half-acre plot,
on a nondescript street
up from the woods
that would soon be cut
to build more and more
of the plain charmless
boxes that crammed
the lost Philadelphia
middle-class suburban
tract where I was raised,
an asleep community
that lacked name, past,
identity other than
transitional and sad.

II

THE SUN'S FAR TASK

Say our world
is the full moon
that has broken
and waxed.
No wonder
each day's axe
comes down dark.
Wolves know that.
Their tracks point,
this time, it seems,
to the heart,
that red cask
of hunger, light.

DAYBROKEN

You're so cold,
Dawn whispered.
taking Sun's hands,
wedging them
in the crook
of a knee.

Now do me,
she crooned,
a van cutting
city corners,
lights flashing,
sirens on.

The Bang

Before the blind date, he found himself
confiding he was out to get laid,
be spirited away, and thought how
he never used phrases like *get laid*,
be spirited away, never confided
like that back in the city.

When she walked in the coffeeshop,
he somehow knew—wild eyes, hair, someone
horny—and rose to take her arm,
nibble her ear. "I'm hungry," he whispered,
"and I want you tonight." And thought how
he never whispered, never wanted.

They drove to her place, a small cabin
in woods near a lake. When he kissed her
throat, she mentioned her boyfriend,
and not being interested—but maybe
in a spell. So they drank wine, flirted,
strolled to the water. He never thought

she'd suggest the skinnydipping, a race
to the raft. He tore out of his clothes,
dived, quickly swam to the platform,
then lay for a moment, his penis pointing
to the waning moon. He never felt her
weight on the creaky board, her body

atop him, firing like a spaceship,
the two suddenly off in orbit beyond
gravity, quick whirling friction
freaky and dark as Pluto, a fit
that cracked and splattered the galaxy
like a box of dropped eggs. Never

such sex, never such a bang
until they duplicated the effort later,
sometime near dawn. He slept emptily,
woke full of air previously unopened,
the shadow family she bore him to.
Never had he risen so far away. Never.

ON THE TRAIN TO THE BIG CITY

From Philadelphia
to New Hope they danced
jitterbugging down the bar car aisle
as twin fiddles swung
jazz. When she kissed his cheek
he looped-the-loop
through New Orleans, azaleas
blooming, a jambalaya of trumpets
pianos and drums.
In his ear
the moon's tip
whispered riverboats
Canal Street
French Quarter lullabies.
She let him mess her hair
and hands clasped
they two-stepped up the corridor.
At Newark they took seats.
And the train swayed
and swayed.

RED PEPPER STIR FRY

For dinner I open sesame
oil, pour into a wok. Once oil
smokes, a quick sizzle when I toss in
minced garlic, ginger, a sliced onion,
red pepper strips curled like barrettes,
cauliflower and broccoli, snow peas,
a peeled carrot. As I mix vegetables,
add sherry, soy, five spices powder,
you set the table: plates, chopsticks,
candles, wine. On the stereo,
old-time Ozark fiddling, a side
of scratchy breakdowns, syrupy waltzes,
a ragged schottische. I dish
bright red, green, orange, white
over rice. Eating, we talk
about couples getting together,
couples breaking up, people going
nowhere. Suddenly I rise from my seat,
lift you, carry you to bed, loving
how your arms wreathe me.

Past midnight, stroking each other's
bellies and breasts, humming
mountain tunes, we spoon ice cream
into each other's mouths, open
fortune cookies. Mine: *Smile*
when you are ready. Yours: *Love*
is a narrow bridge—cross quickly.

VALENTINE'S EVE

To draw the face, start with the eyes. They're blue
and bright, cat-quick yet still. The blue of light
coming up from deep-water dive. Or light
flying down from sky's further gate. The blue
of bird egg, the hatching almost through. Blue
of mirror in woods, the way winter light
plays catch with ice. Blue of steady nightlight
and dreamlight, child's memory room. Blue
times two. Then a quick sketch of nose, mouth, lips.
Linger on the hair, brown curls asking why,
why not, why. That easily the evening slips
away, blinking. Tomorrow arrives with a sigh,
a softening. As if turning everything
into new work, growth. As if gardening.

WHEN MEAT WAS MEAT

1920, when meat was meat, when retirees
in St. Pete, Florida's sunshine town,
played a mean cutthroat shuffleboard
at Mirror Lake, when the century
was rickety rickety as a cable car
climbing some San Francisco street,
her eyes shone, my grandma, prettiest
female sweet in the history of Benjy's
Fine Time Cajun Cuisine, her eyes
like opals the moment she spotted him,
her oldest dream, a real Frenchman,
dashing out of that Louisiana rain
to take an open table in her section,
this young man, my grandpa, who ordered
gumbo and jambalaya both, singing
he had found the queen of queens,
her honeyed breath layering the neatest,
freshest, best-looking, most perfect helping
of whiskey-bread pudding he'd ever seen.

WEDDING SOUP

Begin with dark thoughts. Add
bones, curtains, shoes, a sliver
of spiderleg to taste.
Throw in chickens without heads,
dolls with belly buttons,
toys in boxes. For extra
strength, sprinkle a few whispers,
several riddles, a sly bit
of nowhere. Simmer the mix
in factories between butcher shops
and schools. When set to eat,
assemble the world, and serve
with hunger, two spoons, a secret.

Satan Found!

As you drove east
into Missouri, I read
headlines, skimmed
the outlandish columns,
then told you how
last October Jack Miracle
of Sulphur, Oklahoma
watched a bull moose leap
barbed wire to mate
with Esmerelda, his mare,
and how after naming the foal
Satan, Miracle castrated it,
stating: God told me to.

I thought you'd laugh—
you know, tabloids
as bible. But no. Sober
eyes still on the road,
you said, "Honey, I want
your baby." The next moment
wisps of smoke rose
from the steering wheel—
and the car went dead.

THE VACUUM LADY

A woman with a vacuum
cleaner knocked and asked
if she could. She had
swimmer's shoulders
and a moustache. How much,
I asked. She shook
her head and wheeled
the Hoover inside, the end
of the cord dragging
like a tail. Then she plugged
the machine in, running it
over the rug, the furniture,
me. When I got sucked through
the crack, through the ugly
hairy rollers, I died,
and my death was like my life.
Everywhere, the grinding. Everything,
dark and soft. An invisible
dirty wind. Trapped,
miserable inside a bag
of beat-up furniture, of filth
and litter, I had no idea
who to blame. The vacuum lady?
But that was impossible.
She was doing her job.
As I was mine.

THE END

As you lie in bed reading
Rilke in German, I can tell:
stuck and homesick—
you want change. Sweetheart,
believe me. I am the same.

When I put my hand on yours,
you close the book, kill
the light, turn your back,
pretend to sink into sleep.
Tomorrow we must talk.

COUNTER-WIT

Your problem,
she told him,
is you want
everyone to be
like you.

And yours,
he told her,
is you are.

HOT SPRINGS ROAD TRIP

Despite leaky radiator, a flat,
the seven miles of highway
washed out by flood, the squabble
about where to pitch the tent,

Saturday's burnt breakfast,
the clouds, my sprained big toe,
your wrist gashed by barbed wire,
the dead horse by the river,

the sad cowboy who insisted
we match him beer for beer
because it was the anniversary
of both marriage and divorce,

we enjoyed a night of planets
and stars, a banana moon,
a short steamy weekend away
from struggling to make it work,

before finally calling it quits.
We drove the five hours back
singing bumpy country duets
off-key and through tears.

SMITH'S WALTZ

A phrase here, there,
familiar, not, inevitable,
yes, like sewing a quilt
of sound, nearly square,
nearly, yes, little
variations repeat, yes,
small story of mood
not plot, small story,
not, not anything
but an improbable cloth
that maybe pleases, packed
notes that tease, that knock
one another, a sack
of notes, yes, that pleases,
not, because the odd note
that may not please
makes the phrase
fingers, feet, or ears,
yes, must have, yes,
to feel complete.

SPASMS

Out one Sunday, a twitchy eye met a quick cough. Attraction or distraction, neither could tell, and shyly the two fell in with each other, circling the lake twice.

They had much to discuss—pasts so much alike, they lived in the same part of town, worked similar jobs, had similar acquaintances. They took leave that afternoon, a date to walk the lake the following week.

The next Sunday went much like the previous, though now they recognized each other, knew what to expect, were more relaxed, that twitch and cough. Soon they were meeting two, three, four times a week to circle the lake, hike small hills, explore new trails.

A season passed. And another. Until twitch and cough fully disappeared into one another, like a marriage of salt and squeak, of fickle and gruff. A mingling of the difficult and stubborn with the small and sad.

Oh, impossible earth.

III

THE NIGHTMARE YEAR

I spent one New Year's Eve pacing
grief-stricken for myself, my past
vanishing—where, why, I had no idea
but the awful shuddering emptiness
of each moment broke like a collision
between iceberg and ship. Crushed,
I climbed upstairs, stripped, fell
to bed moaning, and felt my soul jump
from a twenty-story mid-city rooftop.
Wings mangled, my remains splattered
sidewalk. I slept five minutes, woke
panicked: I'd dreamed a brick wall
had come down, thousands of bricks,
every last one toppling on top me,
and I was no more, nothing,
not even a speck, not even spirit.
Bereft, I saw no escape
save a new calling as missionary
who'd give the self wholly to God,
the omnipotent father, and to Church,
the faithful, patient, loving mother.
That calmed me—no longer orphaned,
I prayed the good Lord would take me,
a good child, and let me serve Him.
Thus, the nightmare year had begun.

HOUSESITTER

First night, awake
at two, shaking,
his tension an owl
snatching a trout, he lay

taut and catatonic
past dawn, sporadic sobs
and moans no antidote
for an insomnia that blasted

thirty-six lost years
to the surface, named
the jellyfish and shark
that swam his bowels:

the spineless one that stung
and squeezed; the nasty one
with jaws that snapped;
the mismatched pair

that parented by mating
slime and blood,
deep creatures reduced
to migraine and rape.

Next day, a neighbor
knocked loudly to complain:
The girlfriend's crying—
or was it the lovemaking?—

had kept him up;
could something be done?
Her brother was clawed
to death, the housesitter

explained, quick to dismiss
that homeless time of grief
and fright with a truth
that silenced them both.

CURE FOR TENDONITIS AND ANXIETY

For too long those itsy twinges
and uneasy tweaks have strained
a frantic panicky heart. Relax.
The next spasm or ache that threatens
to pull you headlong down
that vast unnameable swirl
will hurt, not kill. Inflammation's
curse—your life's work must wait.
For relief think neither of an uncertain future
nor the haunted past. Instead,
rely on friends until you must leave
even that last trusted ally,
then set out for a place
of primal and powerful beauty.
There, camped at some spot
near water and trees,
you'll hear a trapped timberwolf's
tortured howl: crippled for life.
For your truth to be otherwise,
you must slay, butcher, eat that wolf.
Only then may you walk home free,
this test of nerve your prelude
to a richer happier life.

Phantom Pain

Like an amputee driven batty
by constant achy reminders
that the missing limb
somehow has been rewired
with what seems a sinister
metaphysical switch, you and I,
whole in parts, have suffered
similar cutting to spirit.

If only we could catch
that detached energy shooting
electricity through the air,
we might not have to bear
our own nowhere pains,
the anxieties triggered
by phantom souls whispering—
grow, grow, grow, grow.

GODIVA'S NIECE

Because she died each June
on her birthday, the girl learned
what her friends couldn't: how
to fall like a cat, hang
like a hummingbird, disappear
and reappear like the moon,
be visible as oxygen.
The time she remained drowned
through August, she watched
from above as the world
watched her float. She woke
that thirteenth year on horseback,
the light spirit atop palomino.
And galloped for the sky.

Are We Not High

A shoeless buddha lords
an earth that has leaked
every green thing—ink,
orchards, oceans—for auto-
mobiles refuse to die, leaving
that hard work for people.
Shoes Buddha Shoes, I've heard
some youngsters say, emerging
barefoot from men's and ladies' rooms,
smoke trailing, and they were only
half-joking. Are we not high,
I watch myself write, matching
inner to outer, catching
myself mid-thought. Oh lord,
I think. We're crying.

THE DISEASE OF THE DISEASE

"Oh God," the therapist blinked,
at last face-to-face
with what came from the glass:
grave eyes, inflamed nose,
an atlas of wrinkles and lines,
the most awful mouth—
like some tongueless devil
struggling for speech.

In grad school she'd learned
not to say "soul" or "heart"
but "the soul of the soul"
or "the heart of the heart"
and double-stuffed her head
with reams of xeroxed clutter.
The therapist was childless,
divorced, a middle-aged

professional whose work
now felt useless and windy
as a leap off a bridge.
She needed her tumor
as she'd once needed her ex:
to peel more layers
as she healed the unspeakable
still raking the depths.

AUTO-IMMUNE

for Sue

Rather than have a spleen removed,
the prednisone refilled, the emergency room
rescue you some frozen midnight when blood
won't clot, take two thousand dollars
from the bank, visit an art store, buy
every tube of red paint, then every tube
of white you can afford. Home, squirt
the oils on bare floor, pick up
a brush, and slop the blank walls
with rows of self-portraits, each body
and face bigger, redder, wilder
than the last, always knives for eyes,
fangs for teeth, wet wounds for hands.
When you've so remade every surface
of the house, take off your clothes,
cut your hair, and slather yourself red.
The disease will be consumed by its color.

WHITEWASH

It was like being shot in the gut
by her father, how her teacher/lover,
the brilliant political science professor
whose abandon in bed foreshadowed
that last glorious New Year's fucking,
rolled off, packed, and announced
he had a plane to catch and would see her
in class next quarter. By the way,
he'd given her a B. Then he was gone.

Next evening she bought white paint
and a brush. Right off, his bedroom.
Then his kitchen, living room, bath.
All night she slopped a first coat
on dark hardwood, fine prints, wallpaper,
windows. Next night she splashed a second.
Leaving near dawn, she breathed deeply
and tipped a last half-full paint can
on his carpet. Then she was gone.

AN ALMOST PERFECT HANGOVER

Some autumn dusk, when every last ghost
casts flat shadows on your living men,
pop the cork off a long bottle
of sparkling wine, pour into glasses,
and toast yourself for having survived
nearly thirty-seven years. How often
the ghosts threatened, lied, tried stealing
you from self. Cheers, you say,
the voice from your still-intact core.
Then you sip from one glass, the other,
back and forth as the sickle
of a moon rises. How those light bubbles
turned to oaky bright clarity,
then turned to the bruised red past.
Feeling crappy next morning, you vomit,
not unhappily, your long-stomached dead men.

NIGHTCLUB RESTROOM

Some Saturday midnights it comes
to this: some off-key lead-singing
rock-and-punk guitar hero stuck
doing lewd things with his groin
thinking he's the next Jim Morrison.
You're there reading the graffiti
by the urinal wondering why oh why
you're spending another drunk hour.
You might as well be in a penitentiary,
or the downstate mental institution
your mother lives. You might as well
be dead. The infected cut on your hand—
better swab it with hydrogen peroxide
once you get home, if you ever do.
If you're reading this, you're hallucinating,
you read on the wall, as you zip
your pants, stumble out toward the music,
the bar, the next two-dollar beer.
Ah, you think. The night has potential.

Peter Pan En Route

His mother never told him
there would be desperate
one-armed men out to harm him,
metaphoric cavemen to bury him,
that the world could be all

rattlesnake-desert beneath lonesome
Jesus sky, that the only true
perfect cherry blossoms budded within
the haze of those late-night
mushroom and peyote flights.

DRIVING WYOMING ON THREE LINES OF SPEED

Patrick's beside me, front seat, going "Damn
Listen to That." I nod and turn the knob.
Rock and roll slams out the back speakers.
Patrick slaps my knee and laughs. "You know what?
I think you're a goddamn Jew for making me
pay half gas when I turned you on to this
crystal meth. This is good shit. Not watered down
a fucking iota."
                I turn to Patrick
who I picked up four hundred miles ago,
thumb out in mid-Nebraska, big backpack.
His faces freezes for a millisecond
as he slaps my knee again. "You're disgusting,"
he says. "Just disgusting. You remind me
of an army buddy who got blown up
at Dix. Fucking Dix. So what do you say?
Pull over. I want to turn you on to more
of the shit. We need to get to <u>Salt Lake</u>. Fast."

IV

RAILROAD DAYS

for Scott Sparling

In the Salt Lake railyard
on what would be our lone trip,
Harp told me why he bummed
the country, criss-crossing
from Lansing to Pine Bluff,
Corvallis to Pensacola:
inside a locomotive, he died
nightly in his dreams,
and the end was like a free-
falling upward, a high dive
flight toward the stars—
and how one night he dreamed
he lay flat on the rails,
the Amtrak Empire Builder
approaching, its whistle
like something out of Genesis,
and it was that roaring
engine that called: *Harp, change
your life—heaven is everywhere
the next freight train goes.*

BABS

A steady December downpour
rots curbside snowbanks
as Babs crosses Franklin Street
slush, pulls open the door
to the Alaskan Bar,
nods to Diz, day manager
and current beau.
6 p.m. Friday, one year
too long in Juneau, Babs—
all legs, red hair,
and freckles; utterly sick
of malcontent state-workers,
low-tipping ass-grabbing
politicos, ornery capital-city
drunks—flicks on
her quick barmaid grin,
fits behind the counter
to relieve Franz, and pours
the first shot of whiskey for luck,
the second for hope.

An eight-hour shift,
she'll duck out at 10—
leaving the bar shorthanded
(no sub in town to trust
not to gossip on this caper)—
to catch the ferry north.
Anchorage-bound, a new man
waiting, she's stuffed
Diz's shower curtain
and mildewy sleeping bag
in her trunk—
Juneau souvenirs.

ADRIFT

Now I understand. Having lost child
and wife, hometown and house,
I love my life like I love the gray
northern sea I know nothing of.

An eider speaks to me in my dreams.
So does a spruce. Last night the ghost
bird honked: Swim. The ghost tree
groaned: Buy a sailboat and learn.

I woke knowing I must trust wind
and water. I'm selling everything.
A friend has a craft I can live on.
The icy depths will teach.

THE ARCTIC DESERT

The cold freezes
history. Melt it,
then mix with vodka.
It stings going down.
That's the truth,
the natives say.
Snow, like white space,
equals time. The air
crackles with stories.
God has looped sun
inside ice and tied
a figure eight.
Chew through it.
The taste takes
getting used to,
like infinity.
That's the truth,
the natives say.

AT LESTER BOOTOOGOOLUK'S

After setting pack on filmy floor,
tuning the fiddle, droning a few,
I sat drinking instant coffee
with Lester, glanced at the woodstove,
then the big day-glo poster
of Jesus—the only decoration
on cracked wall—then out the window
at village landscape equally surreal:

a few flat gravel acres between cliff
and sea, the nomadic compound
for six-hundred Siberian Yup'ik
Eskimo prisoners of birth.
I asked my host why a woodstove
on tundra island. He shrugged.
"Sometimes heater's broke," he said.
"And sometimes lots of good drift."

After visiting students, teaching class,
I knocked on three wrong doors
as I wandered back to Lester's,
in my gut a sudden long sharp ache,
like a just-swallowed sword.
"Game on TV—Cowboys the best,"
Lester greeted my return.
Next commercial break, he rummaged

a side room strewn with walrus tusk,
whale bone, a pile of boxes
in which, he said, were stored his best
old artifacts. Returning, pulling
his chair beside mine, he spilled
a half-dozen toenail-sized chips
on the table. "Your choice," he said.
"I don't know," I said. "Take one,"

he commanded, so I fingered a smooth
bony shard, like a layer of tooth—

and pocketed it. "Next time bring beer,"
Lester said, sweeping the other pieces
to his palm. "I'll tell people. Party."
"Sure," I said, wondering if I should,
then spread my sleeping bag out
between woodstove and television,

later woke dreaming of a drunk Eskimo
stabbing himself in the belly.
I stumbled groaning to the bathroom,
squatted on the bucket, let go
something gruesome and bloody
that smelled like long-held fear.
I later buried Lester's gift at the runway.
Then felt his Jesus leave me as I flew.

ON ABORTION

You won't consider it, will you,
good Christian woman, missionaries'
daughter, battler of perversion
and filth. Twice-divorced
from two abusive men, newlywed
to a hellraising Eskimo storekeeper
who, six months into it, spits
on you, you live with your natural son,
your husband, and your two step-children
cramped inside a tiny house,
a tiny village, an impossible wilderness.

And now one more's due. Shaky
to begin with, you'll beam through pain
and deliver a girl nine months to the day,
this next child a world-champion
screamer. But wait. Your past nightmares
will seem like nothing when number three
slaps you the first time, then slaps harder,
again and again, for not shutting up
the little monster he never wanted.
Nowhere to flee, how you'll fall, woman,
one more sheep in God's master plan.

ACCIDENTAL

One, two, three generations
of darkness, past the edge

of what might be called coma,
he held his breath, and leapt.

That part of him hovered
like a wee invisible hummingbird

beside his left ear. Outside,
after the great large jarring crunch

and crash of the impact—
all that metal reinventing—

a strange quiet
that even the big wind and its howling

couldn't dent. His body stopped,
until just as he'd slipped out,

he slipped back in, shook
his head, touched it, whirled,

and groaned that he was hurt,
forehead bleeding wherever he felt,

what had happened he didn't know,
only that he'd wrecked

at the intersection of old life
and new.

RESCUED

Just when I'd hunkered deeper
into my down bag, readying
to survive what I knew
would be a tortuous night,
our snowmachine posse arrived,
five engines roaring their men-music
uphill to crash site. Quickly
the rescue party examined us,
strapped our gear to the machines,
led us off that unnamed hill
where wind just blew. Head achy,
I gripped the side bars, and rode,
taking in all that was mortal.
"Beautiful country," I yelled
one moment when the motor slowed,
that yell as weak as a pup's yelp.
Still, the ride *was* beautiful,
what ice, sky, and back
of the driver's parka I could see
in the blur, my damaged eyeglasses,
like a compass, in my breast pocket.

RELEASED

Forty-eight hours after I'd risen
from the backseat of the snowmachine
and shakily walked into the hospital,
a man and woman lifted me from bed
to wheelchair, then wheelchair into van,
then down onto the asphalt, then up
the steep stairs onto the jet plane,
then out of that chair and into my paid seat
beside an escort. People gawked:
how often did a black-eyed, bloodied,
bandaged, new-made cripple land in their midst.
So this is to be an old queen, I thought
two hours later, having been transferred
back to chair, then lifted down the stairs,
then wheeled toward, into, and through
the Anchorage terminal. Neck in a brace,
I didn't dare turn, just stared straight,
glimpsing a periphery of eyes. Later,
past midnight, told by an ER doc,
as he roughly undid my plastic collar,
that I didn't need the neurosurgeon
because the CAT Scan showed I'd suffered
no fractured vertebra, I felt happily
intact, a fat oyster with pearl.
"You're on your own for a place to sleep,"
he said, signing the forms, then tossed me
ointments as he glanced at my face.

THE FOG

As if the bad weather
that helped cause the crash
had been slowly siphoned
into me, five days later,
well enough to stand,
I found myself lost
from my usual self.
"Foggy," I said as if
the word explained an exact
invisible solid nothing
fence, the dull knives
of air that separated me.

While Nome enjoyed
long sun-filled days,
little wind, I suffered
thick fog trampling
like ghost moose or bear.
"Foggy," I'd say then,
warning the big beasts.
"We need you," I heard.
"Hush," I'd say next,
sharply, but with love,
being obliged to mind fog
this short while more.

Shadow Man

Seemingly normal, the man—
shadow man, I later named him—
had camped at my table an hour,
and talked. Perhaps a fraction off,
I thought, as he gabbed on
about how he spent his days
listening to radio, watching TV,
and though he'd like to support me,
he wouldn't because he couldn't
read poetry, and had no cash.
I read him a poem, which he liked,
then another, which he claimed
he couldn't fathom. Couldn't
read poetry, or didn't want to,
I challenged. He said he'd taught
psychology a decade earlier,
before his car accident. Now,
after nine years of rehab,
he could sometimes be alone and out
for short periods, could even read
newspapers, save the editorials.
Then he smiled his smile,
like a dog performing a trick.

When the neuropsychologist
diagnosed me with minor head injuries,
I thought of him, my shadow man,
and guessed we'd have intersected
for life in the same dusky fuzz
if I'd have been traveling
a mile or two faster, or if
the nose of the plane had been tipped
a degree or two up. Or down.

DELICATE

I've heard Southern women called *delicate*,
guessing it meant they loathed to perspire.
Funny word, *delicate*. We can admire
the sensitivity. But to commit
to tragic humidity is a bit
of a stretch. What's wrong with sweat? If a choir
sounds delicate, it lacks vital fire.
Delicate state senators better quit.
After the fog from my plane crash lifted,
I entered my delicate phase. I mean
it was as if my brains had been shifted
twenty degrees left. Or as if they'd been
cut and sandwiched. As if I'd just come down
from being sucker-punched once, twice stomped on.

DAVE'S GHOST

Almost two and a half years past
the suicide, I caught you a moment
in the eaves of a story—a friend's
elderly father about to shake hands
the first time with a new neighbor,
watched as that new neighbor, stricken,
somehow keeled over, dead. Dave,
I imagined you presiding, wry crab
that scuttles distance and time.
Coyote host to the lost.

The next week, a thousand miles south,
I heard another story, of a sad man
who'd baked bread, set four loaves
on the counter to cool, then walked
out his cabin that early March evening
to shoot himself in the head.
At the memorial, mourners sliced
and ate the loaves, those hard
dusty crumbs the grain of saltwater,
woods, haunted and wistful fiddle tune.

FOUND ON KODIAK

Atop a Middle Bay ridge,
violet twilight, west peaks
no longer shiny—time
I decided. Some options: North
to shore, a haven of sand
and rock by bay; further north
to town, lights, a ferry
due tomorrow; west
to campsite that promises
fire, food, a tentative partner-
ship with birds; further west
to mountains, now haloed
by wisps. Tired, hungry,
I knew I no longer knew—
and would never know—where
I stood. I only knew this:
surrender. What relief
to know deliverance neared
no matter what direction
next. I unzipped my pack,
found the water, drank
the last. Recapping
the bottle, I watched
clouds crown darkening peaks
far west. I began hiking
that way, happy, alive
having chosen for the night.
Sometime soon I'll reach camp.
When flames catch I'll sing.

V

The Quilter

See how I've stitched white horses
in three corners, a black sheep
in the fourth? A coiled gold snake
from the sheep to a red box
with a raccoon in the middle?

I can tell you this quilt
is for my eldest, in jail for god knows.
I can tell you this piece of cloth
is salvation. It says what I can't.
Says what I must.

IN THE BACKWOODS

By oil lamp and woodstove, an elder knits
a baby's blue wool sock. Her veiny hand
shakes. This first great-grandchild is unplanned—
her favorite granddaughter's, the one who sits
and listens. The great-grandmother-to-be spits
out her chew, sets down needles. She'd once planned
Asia, Africa, the South Sea Islands.
Kids instead. Kids. Five itsy-little bits
who'd filled her life but good. Once she'd been
to Florida. Once to Maine. Once she saw
Bob Hope. Once a famous Irish piper.
Mostly it was cooking, cleaning, staying in,
waiting. Her granddaughter would learn the law
soon enough: write off travel, change the diapers.

NARCISSA'S DIET

She loved artichokes,
how it made her think
of her long fingers
around her little brother's
prickly neck. She hated
brussels sprouts, those
tiny cabbages, her
baby sister's dolls.
On pizzas, always
Canadian bacon, because
she was a sophomore,
a cheerleader-to-be,
and her girlfriends
thought bacon cool.
For dessert, always
chocolate ice cream,
a deep brown swirl
like her own pretty eyes.

TRISH'S SENIOR SPRING, RALEIGH, N.C.

Last night when Victor, her best friend's steady,
brushed her bare left shoulder, she shivered
and felt her heart blush redder than lipstick
and nail polish combined. Much much better
than leading cheers or stealing a smoke,
she'd felt his fingers linger on skin a second
and burn like a brand. Oh god, Samantha
will kill me, she knew, and knew it
sure as her locker, or her biology text
(which she'd taken to reading to tune out
old boring Mr. Wendell), knew it sure as next fall
freshman year at Duke. She shook her blonde hair,
studied herself in the upstairs bathroom mirror.
You're so pretty, she whispered, kissing
the glass, then laughed at her seal
as she bounded down the steps, out the door,
amd onto the driveway, dad's keys jangling.

When a Young Adult Leaves Home, It is Passage

In the Carolina Piedmont, a grandmother,
her three daughters, and seven grandchildren
live in a big white house that needs
repainting. Two backyard trailers, gleaming
in the sun like just-washed railroad cars,
are the teenagers' sleepers.

Only one's ever been gone—the eldest
girl, years ago, California. Educated
at Berkeley, a music major, a singer,
each spring she seeds the flower garden
so August she can gaze from a distance
at green, yellow, black, yellow, blue—

the Tanzanian flag. Just a kid
when she left, she returned pregnant,
carrying the baby of a white man.
Her boy, now seventeen, a cellist
and composer, has won a scholarship north.
He's been raised to never come back.

THE CRUEL GRANDMA

The green apple ought to have
wrinkles, dry gray hair
in a bun, a wistful Iowa
smile with a gap between
chipped front teeth, an apron
dotted with flowers, hands
smelling of gingerbread,
chocolate, and sunshine,
not be the Granny Smith
of winter, the tart apple,
rock-hard and crisp, the one
to hurl through glass.

CLASS OF '77

A decade since I last saw
my college best buddy,
Chuck, mechanical engineer
and doper who graduated
to building nuclear reactors
in Southwestern badlands.
We were smoking in his truck—
I was passing through town—
when I asked how was work,
so he spun the steering wheel
to show off the site, drove
the fifty miles of Utah
nowhere backcountry blacktop
past canyon after canyon
to the spot where the monoliths
rose as mutant cauliflowers
and parsnips, where the hardhat
and lunchpail begot super-uranium
and heat, where we listened
in stupendously crucial silence
to an old Grateful Dead tape
until Chuck said: "My job, pal."

FASHION MODEL

Her slinky beauty makes even bean-counters blink,
challenges handsome men to make themselves handsomer,
possesses asshole dates to paw all over her.
Like an emerald dropped in a kitchen sink
she'll dispense a carelessly quick nod or wink
to this man or that, thinking it's rather
cross that men don't know how to handle her
when all she wants is to simply eat and drink,
act normal and friendly. Instead, rivals
whisper she's anorexic, has an attitude,
is an iceberg, a slut. Whisper she's liable
to be copping coke, crack, speed, ludes,
junk. Just the usual industry gossip.
Common as leather, chain, handcuff, whip.

CHARLENE

Little Orphan Annie hair
and over six feet, pretty
like the grain of sanded
redwood, Charlene blew alto
for the local blues band:
Johnny Wipe and the Vipers.

There were rumors: Charlene
was a dyke, a junkie,
had punched out one ex-lover,
knifed a second. Then her belly
grew. One night, tackling
a mean Charlie Parker riff,

she blew, and from the hole
of the horn a boy and girl
dropped, wailing, their skin
the brown of polished mahogany.
Charlene's sax was spirited.
The twins took the world.

THE SQUARE ROOT OF WEDNESDAY

Accordingly, if Wednesday
is prime, the answer is midnight,
a smoky bar, a woman wearing
a gold bracelet inscribed VERTIGO.

If Wednesday is divisible, punch
through the years until you reach
the dark March day your mother
fought your father to a stalemate,
smothered him in curses that curdled
the house like boiled yogurt.
How they made you gag on gallons,
forcing you fatter and fatter.

If Wednesday is one, the answer,
dreamy mathematician, is to multiply
by Sunday, and divide by self.

TWIN FIDDLES

In a far corner, trading tunes,
you played one I knew;
I followed softly, filling
the odd note. How you looked
at me. I set fiddle and bow
away, made you lay down
yours, took hands. Leading,
I waltzed you in a circle,
swung you into a loop,
kissed you. How you licked
your lip, smiling, our bodies
pretzeled. Next, you hummed
the lullaby that broke me.

RECEPTIONS

Steady quarterback, my grandfather
neatly led me the length of the yard
in soft safe spirals as I ran down-and-outs
and quick buttonhooks against the shadows.

Fourth and goal, my grandfather drilled me
the instant I cut left, and I fell backwards
into the shrubs for a touchdown, the point
of the ball in my belly like a bone,

the pain like a load of breath
sucked through a vacuum. "Hurts so good,
doesn't it," he chortled on and on
like a kid my age, his voice nothing

and everything. Like mine these nights,
being made to catch word after word. Loving it.

To Move

for Suzanne

When I visited Seattle this summer,
though you had a clean carpet, a car
that ran, an adorable boy, a big garden,
you lacked what pleased you most: time

to paint, a lover you craved, that sense
of urgency. Come on. Remember how
that bumblebee hovered and buzzed
by the windowpane before suddenly diving

for that gold snapdragon's blossom?
We wondered: Why that snapdragon? Why
that instant? Come on. Be that bee.
Or, better, start collecting boxes

and be the heroine of this whimsy. Weigh
a certain box; calculate volume; sniff
the dark cardboard air. Then climb in
and disappear with your son. Go now.

KENTUCKY FIDDLE MUSIC

for Bruce Greene

They're out there, fiddlers
like Salyer, Hawkins, Fulks,
Phelps—the fiddling
descendants of fiddling
great-uncles, grandpas,
grannies—fiddling tunes
mournful and disturbing
as that late May frost
twenty-one years back
that ruined poplar
roots. The bowing dies
unless it's passed.
So you learn.

But what of those
you missed. Boley Tolan
of Vortex, Ida Stout
from near Eighty-Eight,
1st Sergeant Phineas Owens
of Shoulderblade, and so on—
their fiddling silenced.
And what of the ones
those you missed
would have pointed.
The journey to source
is an endless drive
into hollows and hills.

PENTAGON

The fifth mountain out
of town. A diamond

with one point
amputated.

A flattened bullet.
A rusted anvil

top. The silvery
microscopic heart

of a computer.
A building

that cannot be
defended.

Home plate.

VI

One More Man in a Furniture Store

Amidst the ottomans,
the sofas, the ugly divan
she quickly dubbed
furniture from Pluto,

he leaned into a fancy
maroon recliner—
this his usual posture—
and cracked a good joke
about upholstery

to prove some point
before creaking
a few short creaks,
and disappearing
into the wood.

My Father's Gift

After hiking uphill seven miles,
a fifty pound pack strapped to my shoulders,
I napped in a lean-to beneath a spruce,
and dreamed of Baker, the high, white mountain
I always dreamed. The dream never changes.
Three quarters up the north face, I fall in
a crevasse, a partner watching me go.

I woke at dusk, disoriented, tense.
My shelter smelled leafy, wet. I crawled
to damp dirt, sat on a damp log, shivered
as wind shook rain from alders. I unzipped
my pack, fumbled for a cap and the book
brought this camping trip, the bible my dad
sent me last October, a month before

his sudden death. I held the book's spine,
fit the cap on my head. Then I flipped pages:
Genesis, Numbers, Judges, Kings—scriptures
that meant nothing. On a shadowy rock
I set the book down, looked, saw a squirrel dig
through a firepit, climb a spruce. Far engines
droned. Closer, I heard two sparrow hawks call

as mates. The grove darkened. A second squirrel
dug through char and ash, climbed. I kicked twigs
into the pit, stooped for sticks and branches
that I tossed on top. Then I reached in my shirt
for a match, lit it, threw it to wood.
Nothing. The tiny light fizzled and died.
I lit one more. Nothing. So I squatted

over the bible, ripped the end pages,
crumpled them in balls that I set beneath
the kindling. Then I struck a new match,
put it to paper. The fire caught. Quickly
I tore more sheets, six, seven at a time,
threw the wads in the fire so bright orange

flared. When the thickest branch ignited,
I dropped the whole bible in the firepit.
First, smoke. Then, chapters curled, covers melted,
the spine fried. I kicked at wet leaves, trembling
as I remembered my father, his foibles,
his fierce loyalty. I'd never loved him, damnit.
And he had loved me so much. I stood there
and watched the book disappear into the air

with a last crackle. That made me weep,
that crackle. I hadn't been a good son,
had been unable to love. Now he was gone.
I pulled my cap over my ears, opened my hands
to the fire's glow, took in the warmth.
I needed small logs to cook a meal. Soup
would fill me, let me sleep, dream further, climb.

OPENING KETCHUP

If you've tapped the top
on the counter, run hot water,
called brute strength to grip

and wrench, and still can't,
don't psychoanalyze the bottle.
Find a more responsive tool:

the cruel raspy voice
undamaged in the debris
from January's killer quake.

Say: Dad, gimme a goddamn hand
to twist this goddamn thing off—
diction like the rumbling

that buckled sunken floorboard.
A father's never too dead to come
uncap what smacks of blood.

DEAD DAD

Dead Dad, I wrote,
not catching the error
until I reread the note.
Changing the *d* to *r*,
I sent it off.

Father, it's been weeks
since that letter
was mailed. Why'd I think
you'd respond? You *are* deader
than I thought,

a ringer for your folks.
Father, maybe you breathe,
eat, tell a few jokes.
But you failed me,
you old corpse.

The Widow

Through dirty windows, she sees the maple
heave, its red and orange leaves fall,
and believes her grief is like that west wind's
bluster—and she is like that maple's bough.
"When will I break," she asks. "I'm tired.
I'm sick. I've had enough. He's been dead
two full years. When will he leave?"

The widow's wrong. Her grief's not that wind—
and she's not a branch about to snap.
If life must be metaphor, let hers be a hanging
gray January sky over prairie, mercury
below zero, the forecast: blizzard.
The west wind's only a playful autumn gust.
Her tree is being primed for the storm.

A View of My Mother

She lay perfectly
still—her cold eyes
and lips, long face
and neck, big bust—
this pitiful mom, raised
by bumblers, ruined
by a dope of a husband
whose witless sewage
she steeped like tea,
who used me to plug
her awful endless hole.
The abuse, which cursed
thirty years, left me
curiously shell-shocked,
a once-bright hope turned
dark fury. Now, finally
forced to pay respects,
feeling the absolute
of the near-forgotten,
I'm summoning nerve.
See how the mortician
set my mother's mouth—
her first smile in years.

A Pillow is Not Glass

You urged me to remember
the rage, to reclaim my core
energy by flexing knees, grounding
bare feet with floor, and talking
ugly about my mother.
A sick bitch, I said,
an old bat I was tired of.
"That sick batty bitch," you shrieked,
wheeling to the corner to grab
a long stick with which you whacked
cushions, a grunt for each hit.
When you handed me a stick,
pointed to a pillow,
dared me to beat the fuck
out of my mother, I snapped.
Asshole Miami psychiatrist, you
and your props. I grew up
smothered in a house
much like your office.
Taunt me with a stick,
I'll break something.
Order me to muffle it,
I'll poke out your eyes.

THE CACTUS HAS BLOOMED PERFECT RED PETALS

I lie like a dog
on the parallelogram
the sun has lit
in the exact middle
of the living room rug.
Though my cheek's
pleasantly baked
and my haunch tingles,
I'd kill that self
to become my blooming
cactus. As the sun goes,
so must I. I'll move
by inches until the room's
all shade. I'll wait
beside the window
until my flowers are dead.

DOLL RITUAL

He found three at a flea market—
the big thick-lipped hyena
in the black-and-white plaid
that only needed a cigar
to look like his father,
the gangly near-Raggedy Ann
with the stringy brown mouth
and hair that so reminded
of his mother, the small
blank unfinished nothing
that might have been him—
and stuck needles in the faces
and feet for a week.

The next Friday afternoon
he drove them to the park,
hiked beyond rocky ridge,
trees, and trail, past a lake
to a far spot where cloud,
sun, and raw February sky
would soon collide with dusk.
Twilight like a purple ship,
he lit a match to the heap
of twigs he'd criss-crossed
like thatch within a circle
of stones, and when fire caught,
fed the little doll

that might have been him
to the flame, coolly watched
the straw innards flare at once,
then disappear with a snap.
Next, the animal, which blackened
almost as quickly, a glob
of something fat, smelly, cruel.
Last, the female, which refused
to burn until he stabbed it
in the chest, threw more sticks
on the pile, poked the embers.
That one crackled until only ash,
wind, and shadow remained.

CHRISTMAS SMORGASBORD

Our upper-middle-class Yules: holiday
vacations skiing Vermont, or playing golf
in Boca, or home watching TV in every room.
The evening tradition: making reservations
and getting dressed to eat at a hotel.
We'd fill plates one, two, three times—
each trip a pile of peeled jumbo shrimp,
scalloped potatoes, corn, a thick slice
of prime rib *au jus*. I noticed
the servers regarded us—four strange people
cut off from family and friends—
pityingly. When my little sister asked
to be excused, the parents said nothing—
one busily chewing, the other wanting more.
After dessert we went our ways until next year.

BENEATH ORANGE SUN

There's some joke circulating
that he's 43. Or is he 42?
One year's the same as the next,
product of empty revision.
His muse, a fallen tooth fairy,
leaves graffiti under the pillow.
He wakes feeling utterly fucked.
His mother's voice says no more.
No more birds, crops, poems.
Crows and cornfields, he types,
ever the disobedient one.

COYOTE BANK

I'd lugged the heavy glass dog
over ten years, encouraging it
with wheat pennies, buffalo nickels,
Mercury dimes, bicentennial quarters
and half-dollars, Susan B. Anthony's,
always imagining one day taking
the bank to a dealer and trading
for crisp bills. Or willing it
to grandchildren, godchildren, perhaps
some charity. Until waking one full moon
summer night with the money banging
and jingling in my head, a creepy nervous
feverish energy telling me to grab
the coyote, go outside to the patio,
and fling it hard, snout-first
onto the concrete, shattering glass,
making every cent crash and fly,
erasing what financial sense my father,
in his depression wisdom, had instilled.
How good the hours after impact felt.
Sweeping the mess, separating shard
from coin, everything shone.